THOUGHTS for the HOLIDAYS

Finding Permission to Grieve

by Doug Manning

In-Sight Books

1st printing–September 2001

Copyright© 2001 by In-Sight Books, Inc.
P. O. Box 42467
Oklahoma City, Oklahoma 73123
800-658-9262 or 405-810-9501
www.insightbooks.com

Manufactured in the United States of America

ISBN 1-892785-40-4

Cover Photo: *Digital Imagery© copyright 2001 PhotoDisc, Inc.*
Quotes: *Forever Remembered–A Gift for the Grieving Heart.*
Compendium, Inc., 1997, ISBN 1-888387-20-3.
and
Staudacher, Carol. *A Time to Grieve–Meditations for Healing After the Death of a Loved One.* HarperCollins, 1994,
ISBN 0-06-250845-8.

In the rising of the sun and
in its going down
We remember them;

In the blowing of the wind and
in the chill of winter,
We remember them;

In the opening of the buds and
in the warmth of summer,
We remember them;

In the rustling of leaves and
the beauty of autumn,
We remember them;

In the beginning of the year and when
it ends,
We remember them;

So long as we live, they too shall live,
For they are now a part of us as
We remember them.

Gates of Prayer
Reform Judaism Prayerbook

Thoughts for the Holidays

*Sometimes, when one person is
missing, the whole world seems
depopulated.*

— Alphonse de Lamarline

It was all she could do to open the door and walk into the party. Her husband, Charles, had died a few months before and now she found herself going to the office Christmas party she could not find a way to avoid. Mary and Charles had built the company together and now the whole burden was on her shoulders. She did not want her grief to rob the employees of their annual party which had always been one of the highlights of the year. The employees always brought their families along so this became a time of bonding together. There were always toys for the children, good food and entertainment.

Mary could not stand the thought of attending this event, but she could not stand the idea of canceling either. The party would be a crushing reminder that Charles was no longer here and would never be here for these events. The joy the party would bring seemed to make light of his death. Laughing and having a good time seemed totally out of place and somehow wrong. Yet she drove to the party, full of dread and anger, but she went.

The first person she met as she walked in the door was her pastor. He was a fixture at these events and was always invited. He grabbed her hand and said, "Mary, the secret is to just be happy." She thought that to be one of the worst platitudes she had ever heard, but she smiled and said nothing. Then she met the pastor's wife who said, "Mary I know this is a hard time for you, but doesn't it give you great comfort to know that Charles will be spending this Christmas with Jesus?" Mary, the dedicated church pianist, heard herself scream "No!! He should be spending it with me." She still blushes when she tells the story, but there is a hint of pride in her voice even as she blushes. That was *exactly* what she should have said.

The husband of another woman died a few months before Thanksgiving. Her children could not stand the thought of their mother being alone for that day and put so much pressure on her that she had little choice. She went to their home for Thanksgiving and had a miserable time. She had no emotions to spare on such things as gratitude and joy. It hurt to be involved in a family event when her husband could not attend. She felt almost dirty for being there and had no idea where those feelings came from. She said she would do the dishes as a way of escape into the kitchen. She forgot that the window over the sink in her daughter's kitchen looked out on the cemetery where her husband was buried. She suddenly burst into tears and screamed, "Why did you leave me like this?" How dare you do this to me." The family overheard her and, of course, could not understand nor could she explain. The holidays had overloaded another grieving person.

The Waves of Grief

*The ocean has its ebbings—
so has grief*

— Proverb

Wherever you are in your grief journey, you have probably found that grief comes in waves that seem to overcome your being. You may have figured out that some of these waves are fairly predictable and seem to almost be on some hidden schedule, while others hit for no apparent reason without warning. Some people say they have been overwhelmed by a sudden wave in the grocery store or some other public place.

Most likely you have figured out that all of the special days in a year bring on a wave that starts about thirty days before the event and builds until the day arrives. The anniversaries of birth, marriage, death or other significant times seem to hit with a vengeance.

Then the Holidays Happen

Those times of great joy and family involvement now must be faced with fear and dread. Christmas, Hanukkah, Thanksgiving, Easter, Mother's Day, Father's Day, and even Valentine's Day all bring on a tidal wave of grief that must be faced and handled with care.

Why do the Holidays Hurt?

On the surface, it is hard to see how the holidays could possibly cause a problem. They are times of great happiness and, to those who have never been through grief, you look like someone who needs some cheering up and a break from your sadness. To others the holidays are family times and it always helps to be around family and friends. That never fails to bring cheer to a lonely heart, so your family and friends will probably be convinced that the holidays are just what you need. They may bring great pressure upon you to join in with enthusiasm so you can get away from your grief for a time of joy. They do not understand that the holidays themselves can create some added burdens and added sorrows.

After the loss of a loved one, the first time you laugh you will most likely feel a twinge of guilt. It will not seem proper. You may feel you are not being true to the memory of your loved one if you laugh. You may well feel you are not honoring who they were nor the seriousness of the loss. The holidays create the same kind of guilt. "How can I dare have fun when my loved one is gone?" may be the message of your heart.

The Significance of Significance

The mind has a dumb sense of vast loss—
that is all. It will take mind and memory
months and possibly years to gather the
details and thus learn and know the
whole extent of the loss.

— Mark Twain

The first thing we want to do, and the first thing we need to do, after a loss is establish the significance of the loss and the person. This is human nature. When bad things happen to us we feel an intense need to tell someone. Matter of fact, we tell several "someones" until we are understood and our loss is noted by others. When the loss has been fully realized we can move on in our journey, but if it is not noticed, or if it is made light of, our journey seems to stall and we cannot move.

There are at least three areas where significance must be established:

First, you need to establish the significance of the person. There is no way to know the value of a person until they are lost. I know I love my wife, but I have no idea what she means to me and I won't know unless she dies first. When a loved one is gone, we begin discovering what they meant to us. Every day will bring to mind some other part of who they were and what they meant. Every day you will think of something you did together, something they said, little traits that made them unique, pet names you used, and new things you want to talk over with them. You will get a deep feeling of closeness with anyone who will talk about the person. Friends may find this difficult and be afraid of hurting you by bringing up the subject, but nothing feels better. The number one need right now is to establish the significance of this person. You want to scream, "Hey world, look at my love and weep with me over my tremendous loss."

Second, you need to establish the significance of your loss. It is almost as if you must inventory the loss before you can grieve it. Now you can understand what needs were met by this love in your life. Too often we take things for granted. We accept love, companionship, friendship, joy, laughter, and peace as just part of living. When they are gone, we inventory those losses and we want the world to recognize how deeply they are missed.

Third, you need to establish the social significance of your loved one. We want to know how much this spouse/parent/child/ or other significant person meant to others. Hearing the praise of the family and friends feels wonderful. They also loved. They also hurt. They also miss. This person and this loss is important. This person mattered and will continue to matter for years to come.

The Holiday Dilemma

Life must go on
And the dead be forgotten;
Life must go on,
Though good men die;
Anne eat your breakfast;
Dan take your medicine;
Life must go on;
I just forget why.
— Edna St. Vincent Millay

Then comes a holiday, and the whole world wants to lay aside all else and have joy and celebrations and religious expressions and gifts and lights and you want to scream, "Not yet!' What about my love? Are you forgetting the loss of my lifetime?" It all seems to trivialize the person and the loss. How could there be celebration? How could there be joy? You are in a desperate quest for significance and suddenly you are the only one interested. The rest of the world seems to be saying, "Put away all of that and come celebrate with us." You can't, and you can't help but feel anger that they can.

Holidays Can Create Conflict

It is easy to see how conflicts can develop. The family and friends want everything back to normal so the holidays can happen. You know there will never be such a thing as "normal" again. They want the holidays to go on just like they always have, you know that holidays *as usual* deny the loss and trivialize the life of your love.

The pressure may become quite intense. "We need the holiday to be normal for the children", or "This is what the person would have wanted." There are many ways to say it, but the message is the same—it is time for you to get past your grief and get things back to the way they were. And that can't be done.

Holidays Interrupt the Grieving Process

Grief is full time work. It dominates every waking moment and demands your full attention and all of your time. This is especially true in the first several months of the process. Grief is transition. Where you are today is not where you will be tomorrow. Every day presents a new set of thoughts and feelings that must be processed. Grief also demands all of the energy you can muster. As a result, you have neither the time nor the energy to give to a holiday. Just thinking of having to make preparations for some family gathering is enough to exhaust you for days.

Grief means you are living on survival level. The only thing you can do is survive each day. You may often feel that you have become a very selfish person and that you are just feeling sorry for yourself, but you are neither. Surviving is not the same as selfishness. Surviving is an inborn defense within each of us that turns all the energy we have inward to protecting our sanity and well being. When our emotional well being is attacked, surviving dominates us no matter who we are or how unselfish our normal lives are. When you are surviving, holidays seem far too trivial to even be considered.

This means the idea of shopping for Christmas presents, preparing for Hanukkah, or attending some family celebration places demands upon you that you just cannot meet. My hope is that this little book will help you realize that and protect yourself without a great deal of guilt.

Holidays Make Demands on us
We Can Not Fulfill

The holidays demand focus you cannot give. You may try, but you will not be able to tune in or concentrate on the holidays. You may well feel like a zombie going through the motions, but the focus will not be there.

The holidays demand emotions you are not able to give. The depression of grief often exemplifies its presence not just by blue feelings, but also by no feelings at all. You feel detached and emotionally dead. You go through the motions, but feel as if you are outside your body watching yourself as you perform, but there is no emotional involvement on your part.

The holidays demand an act that will drain you completely dry. If you allow yourself to be forced into "business as usual" for the holidays, you must put on a smile and an act that is draining of energy you do not have to give. An hour of this act is the equivalent of a long hard day of labor. It is exhausting and you need all of your strength to get through your journey.

The Key to the Holidays is Permission

Joy and pain can live in the same house. Neither should deny the other.

— Tan Neng

If you boil down all the books written, all the speeches given, and all the seminars offered on the subject of grief, they all come down to one important essential concept. People need permission to grieve. It is the key to all progress in the grief journey. It is also the hardest thing to attain.

It is hard to get the permission to grieve from friends and family. They mean well. They want you to be well and happy, but in their zeal they try to trivialize your grief by giving you a new way to think about the loss, or they pressure you to act well long before you are.

I think there is a pattern to how friends usually approach a person in grief:

First they explain. They will fill the air with all kinds of reasons why the loss happened. They seem to know exactly what God had in mind and how He plans to work it all out for the better. Far too often instead of cheering you up, the explanations will break your heart. There is no end to the variations on the explaining as to why bad things happen to us. Almost all of them end up defending God or nature at your expense, and few make you feel better.

Then they argue. If explanations do not work, then the arguments start. "Now you can't let yourself feel that way." "It is time for you to get on with your life." "You need to look at things with a more positive outlook and be glad for the blessings you have." The arguments are even less helpful than the explanations.

Then they criticize. If the explanations and arguments do not get you kick-started into a happy life, then they will begin to criticize. "You aren't trying to get well." "You are just wallowing in your grief." "Do you enjoy feeling sorry for yourself?" I don't even need to comment on how helpful the criticisms are.

I often say, if explanations worked, there should be no more war. If arguments worked, there should be no more divorce, and if criticism was really constructive, I should be perfect.

Permission from others is tough, but giving yourself permission is an even greater battle. A woman said, "Every morning I get up and say to myself. I will not 'should' on me today. I love that. You may well *should* yourself into frustration saying, "I *should* be ready for the holidays." "I *should* do it for the children." "I *should* not hinder the plans of the rest of the family."

It is hard to tell yourself it is all right to be weak. It is all right to not be "over it" by now. It is all right not to enjoy Thanksgiving, or Christmas, or Hanukkah this year. There will be other years. The world will still stand if one season of holidays is missed. It is all right to be the Grinch that stole the holiday this year.

What About the Children?

Of course the question of what to do about the children may come up. Families with children should involve the children in planning for the holidays. Decide together how this season will be done and stay with the plan. Unless the children are very young, and depending on the loss, they may also be in grief and have special needs for facing the holidays. These needs are best met by the family deciding together how this special year will work best.

There are always friends who want to help. Let them do the shopping for the children. If the loss is fresh, the holiday bedecked stores are more than you should have to experience.

Next year you can make it up to the children. They will survive.

Permission To Do What You Can Do

*Most people don't know how
brave they really are.*
— R. E. Chambers

You should feel free to decide what you can do and what you want to do for these holidays. If you have always cooked the turkey at Thanksgiving, you must be free to decide if that is something you can and want to do this year. You also need to think through what you want to do about house decorations, gift giving, parties and family functions. It helps to make a plan in advance and then structure the plan by letting family and friends know exactly what you plan to do and not to do. The structure should not rule you, but it should be complete enough to cover most of the areas you will face. If the family knows in advance, they know what to ask of you. Hopefully they will stay within the boundaries you set.

Permission to be Where You Need to Be

The son of a woman who worked in our office died of suicide. The first Christmas after his death, his parents and sisters went to Disney World. The extended family could not understand and applied almost unbearable pressure for them to not go. They were told that they needed to be together this one year more than ever. They were told that it was selfish to abandon the family at this time. They went anyway. This family had a tradition of making a very big deal out of Christmas and the grieving parents knew they just could not participate that first year. They were smart enough to know the only way out was to leave town.

It is not possible for every family facing loss to go on a trip for the holidays, but you must force permission to be where you are comfortable, and not feel guilty for not being places where you are not comfortable. There may not be any explanation as to why you are comfortable in some settings and not in others, but that will be the experience. For some reason you will be able to relax with certain people and not with others. Often your best friends, or family will not be on the relaxed list. That does not mean you like them less. It does not mean they are doing anything wrong. It just means that right now, you can find safety and peace in one spot and not another. Go to those spots and don't feel guilty about the ones you miss. There will be plenty of time to explain and make up later. Right now you need a safe place to be. Find one and spend the holidays there.

Permission to Change Traditions

When someone I love dies, I buy
a candle. There are twelve across my
mantle now: one for my father, one for
my mother, one for my daughter, two for
my grandfathers, and seven for my babies
who were born too soon.
It is a simple comforting act to
light them in reverent remembrance of
each life. Whenever anyone stops to count
these candles, the question I am most
frequently asked is, "How did you do it?
How did you survive?" My usual answer:
"I don't know."

— Dana Gensler
Twelve Candles
LARGO Newsletter

The family may not understand. But the traditions must change. Every family has their own traditions that often have developed over several generations. These can become almost sacred within the family and there may be great resistance to any changes offered, but some traditions must be either changed or at least put off for a time. For example, if stockings were always hung at Christmas and a child dies in the family, what is to be done about the stockings next Christmas? Hang all of them up and act as if the child did not die? Hang all but one up and call attention to the loss in graphic illustration? Or just quietly let the stockings go for a time? In the future, it may become appropriate to have stockings again but, until then, there must be a change in tradition.

A good rule is—if it hurts, don't do it. If it is so painful that you cannot think about it without reacting, then leave it alone for a time.

Our grandson, Isaac, was born on Christmas Eve and died on Christmas Day. When he died, our Christmas holidays changed forever. As the first one approached I had to try to figure out what was appropriate. What traditions could remain and which ones had to change. We had to figure out how to honor the holidays at the same time we were experiencing the anniversary of his death.

Over the seven years since Isaac died we have evolved our own tradition. Just before the family opens the presents, we pause to remind the family how old Isaac would be and how we would have enjoyed him in the same way we enjoy the other grandchildren. Then a candle is lit in his honor. For the first several years, I always produced the candle and led the service. Gradually the grandchildren have taken on the task on their own initiative. With no prompting from me, one of them will ask if he or she can light the candle. In this small way we keep Isaac alive in our memories and in our family.

Many families plant trees, or find some other permanent memorial that can be shared during this time. You must feel free to change any tradition necessary and to start new ones in honor of the person who has died.

Permission to Relate to God in a Different Way

God is closest to those with
broken hearts.

— Jewish Saying

Part of the problem with the holidays comes from the fact that most of them are based in our religion. When a death comes our faith is also changed. We may not feel the same way toward God as we once did. Many find great solace in prayer, but just as many report that they cannot pray at all. The emotions we once felt when we prayed are shut off or exhausted. Often we feel anger toward God because of our loss.

One woman said, "I lost the magic in my religion. I have gradually rebuilt my faith, but I don't expect magic answers any more." A minister said, "I have told folks that we have angels watching over us and protecting us. Then my daughter was killed. Where was her angel?" These are legitimate and honest questions, and they have a profound impact on our faith.

With all of these thoughts, fears, and emotions filling our hearts, it is normal to expect the holidays to seem hollow and empty. You need permission to be just as religious as you really feel for as long as you feel the way you do. If prayer helps, then by all means pray. If your faith is firm and that is how you get through each day, by all means stand on it. But if you don't find peace there, do not let anyone pressure you into acting like all is well when it is not. God is big enough to take our anger. It is all right to be angry. It is all right to say you are angry. It is all right not to be moved when Christmas carols are sung or during the beautiful celebration of lighting the Menorah. In time you will rebuild your faith. It may be much deeper and more meaningful then than it ever was before.

Permission to Find Safe People

You may forget with whom you laughed, but you will never forget with whom you wept.

— Carie O'Leary

We often talk about grief therapy. In reality there is no such thing. You will not get over your grief because some magic therapy method made it go away. We should not even use the word when we are dealing with grief. We are not healed by therapy, we are healed by companioning. Someone walks with us through the journey. We need a safe place and we need safe people who will just be near us and lend us an ear.

As we talk, we find insight into our emotions and our pain. As we talk, we work though the pain. As we talk, we gradually walk through the valley and learn a new way to cope. You will be healed, not by the working of some program, but by the ears of your friends who simply listen while you grieve.

During the holidays, maybe more than any other time, you will find the comfort of a listening ear to be the one safe place you need to face all of the emotions and pain stirred up by a time that once was the cause of great joy, but now is the reminder of great loss. Find the permission to be safe until these days pass.

"You will not always hurt like this"
These words are true.
If they do not reach your heart today,
Do not reject them:
keep them in your mind.

One morning, not tomorrow perhaps,
but the day after tomorrow,
or the month after next month…
One morning the dawn will wake you
with the inconceivable surprise:
Your grief will have lost one small
moment of its force.

Be ready for the time when you can feel
for yourself that these words
are true:
"You will not always hurt like this."

Sascha
"True Words" Wintersun

Doug Manning

His career has included minister, counselor, business executive, author and publisher. He and his wife, Barbara, have been parents to four daughters and long-term caregivers to three parents.

After thirty years in the ministry, Doug began a new career in 1982. He now devotes his time to writing, counseling and leading seminars in the areas of grief and elder care. His publishing company, In-Sight Books, Inc., specializes in books, video and audio tapes specifically designed to help people face some of the toughest challenges of life.

Doug has a warm, conversational style in which he shares insights from his various experiences. Sitting down to read a book from Doug is like having a long conversation with a good friend.

Selected Resources from In-Sight Books

Don't Take My Grief Away From Me
The Gift of Significance
The Special Care Series
Lean On Me Gently–Helping the Grieving Child
Thoughts for the Lonely Nights journal and CD
Thoughts for the Grieving Christian journal and CD

For a complete catalog or ordering information contact:
In-Sight Books, Inc.
1-800-658-9262 or 405-810-9501
www.insightbooks.com